DATE DUE

SEP 1 3 1995	
NOV 0 2 1996	
NOV 2 7 1996	
DEC 0 4 1997	

DEMCO, INC. 38-2971

FOSSILS
Stories From Bones and Stones

Patricia L. Barnes-Svarney

—an Earth Processes book—

ENSLOW PUBLISHERS, INC.

Bloy St. & Ramsey Ave.	P.O. Box 38
Box 777	Aldershot
Hillside, N.J. 07205	Hants GU12 6BP
U.S.A.	U.K.

To my parents, William and Helen Barnes, who have spent many good hours helping me look for the elusive fossils . . .

Copyright © 1991 by Patricia L. Barnes-Svarney

Library of Congress Cataloging-in-Publication Data

Barnes-Svarney, Patricia L.
    Fossils: stories from bones and stones / Patricia L. Barnes-Svarney
        p. cm — (An Earth processes book)
    Includes bibliographical references and index.
    Summary: Explores the history and formation of fossils, current research relating to fossils, and their importance to the field of paleontology.
    ISBN 0-89490-294-6
    1. Fossils—Juvenile literature. 2. Paleontology—Juvenile literature. [1. Fossils. 2. Paleontology.] I. Title.
II. Series.
QL765.B36   1991
560—dc20   90-19408
                                              CIP
                                              AC

Printed in the United States of America

10 9 8 7 6 5 4 3 2 1

Contents

1

Big Bones of Old

The dinosaur bone fields are desolate, ancient places, constantly exposed to wind and ice and only known to a few people who have braved the cold. But to paleontologists—scientists who study ancient life on earth, especially using fossil evidence—they contain some of the most interesting scientific finds of the past few decades. Bylot Island, Ellesmere Island, and Amund Rignes Island—all in the high Arctic—contain the world's northernmost discoveries of dinosaur fossil bones. These dinosaur bone fields are some of the richest in the northern hemisphere.

Of all the fossils, large bones and hard parts of ancient creatures have made the most lasting impressions. Some fossil bones are from animals that resemble modern ones, such as the *Glyptodon*, a tough-skinned, armadillolike creature 4 feet (1.2 meters) in height that roamed Texas more than one million years ago; or the *Pachydyptes*, a 6-foot (1.8 meter) tall ancestor of modern penguins. The twenty-five-million-year-old remains of the *Pachydyptes* have been found in numerous rock layers in the southern hemisphere. The numerous bones of a sea creature called the *Ichthyosaur*, found in 180-million-year-old rock layers in many places around the world, resemble those of today's dolphins.

What have these fossils revealed to scientists about the past? Through the study of old bones, paleontologists have pieced together the ages, shapes, sizes, and even the walking habits of these ancient organisms—large and small. A fossil bone that is hollow may indicate a flying creature much like modern birds. The hefty front and back leg bones of the ornithischians, a type of dinosaur, may show that they were quadrupeds or animals that walked on four legs. Contrary to previous thought it is now believed that some dinosaurs, based on the mammal-like structures of their ancient bones, may have been warm-blooded.

There was probably no life for at least a billion years after the earth was formed. The oldest rock found so far on the earth is 3.96 billion years old; but it is estimated that the earth and other planets and satellites of the solar system have been around for 4.6 billion years. (To comprehend these large numbers, it may help to note that 4.6 billion seconds equals 150 years!)

The biggest fossils are not the oldest ones. Around 3.2 billion years ago, there were small, single-celled organisms. The first larger shelled organisms lived in the seas around 600 million years ago, and the bigger boned creatures appeared millions of years later. First there were fishes, then the amphibians (organisms that lived in the sea and on land) emerged about 380 million years ago. Then reptiles appeared about 320 million years ago or earlier, with dinosaurs emerging around 200 million years ago. Finally, mammals began to rise in number around 190 million years ago. During these times, small-boned creatures also lived, scurrying from place to place to evade larger-boned predators.

What Is a Fossil?

Almost everything known about the creatures of the past is based on the large and small fossils found in rock layers around the world. The term *fossil* is from the Latin word that literally means, "something dug up." Fossils are the remains of ancient organisms—either flora or fauna—preserved close to their original shape. Examples of fossils are bones, antlers, teeth, shells, and footprints—all of which are often found in ancient rock layers. Some fossils are visible to the naked eye, while others are microscopic in size.

How does a fossil form? As an animal is buried, the soft parts such as fur, flesh, or hair slowly decay, because there is little oxygen to cause rapid disintegration. Hard parts of the animal, such as bones and teeth, usually do not decay as easily. As the sediment builds up, the great pressures from above turn the sediment into rock, with the hard parts becoming compressed by the rocks. After thousands or millions of years, if the rock is broken open or exposed, the hard parts are visible. These parts, or any imprints, are known as fossils.

Some organisms without hard parts often leave fine impressions of their bodies if they have had unusual burials. For instance, ash and dust from a volcanic explosion can rapidly cover a dead organism such as an insect, cutting off oxygen that causes decay. Or, an organism can be quickly buried in black mud where oxygen is absent. These conditions lead to the most complete preservation of such creatures.

Not all organisms leave evidence of once being on the earth. In fact, it is amazing that so many fossils have survived over time, as there are many natural and environmental conditions that can destroy the remains of organisms after they die. For example, it is estimated that of the 3,000 plant' and animal species living in today's coral reefs, only around 75 species are easily recognizable after they die—all because of the way the natural ocean environment reacts on the dead organisms. On land, the reaction is even more dramatic. For instance, if an animal dies on top of the ground, it is exposed to air. Bacteria can completely or partially decay the creature's soft parts; while, scavengers eat away at an animal's soft and hard parts. Chemicals in the water and air can also increase the decay rate of a dead animal. In addition, the hard parts of animals can be broken apart by other animals, or bleached and weakened by the harsh sun.

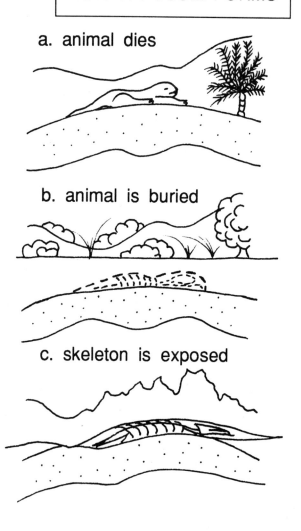

HOW A FOSSIL FORMS

a. animal dies

b. animal is buried

c. skeleton is exposed

A fossil forms when it is quickly buried by sediment and the soft mud turns to stone.

Leaving an Impression

Not all fossils are the hard parts of an ancient creature. Sometimes all that remains is an impression of the animal. For instance, an organism dies and is buried in soft sediment. As time passes, the sediment turns to rock. If the rock develops small cracks, water may seep into the tiny chips within the rock, eventually dissolving the hard parts of the organism and leaving a cavity with only an imprint of the creature. This impression is called a mold.

Animal footprints in rock are types of fossil molds, and are studied by ichnologists—scientists who study ancient footprints. Such tracks indicate whether the animal walked on two legs (a biped) or four legs (a quadruped), how heavy it was, and how fast it was moving. One famous sandstone rock layer along the Connecticut River is filled with dinosaur tracks. One common track was made by a *Brontozoum*, which lived in the Connecticut region 170 million years ago. These tall dinosaurs made numerous foot tracks in the soft mud along the shore

These dinosaur tracks from Connecticut were left in once soft mud. The pencil gives an idea of scale.

between high and low tides. Based on these tracks, scientists believe that the *Brontozoum* walked on its hind legs in search of vegetation.

If a mold becomes filled with minerals or mud, it is called a cast. Often casts are filled with such minerals as quartz, calcite, or pyrite. Small brachiopod casts filled with pyrite are often found in parts of Ohio, and calcite fills the former shells of nautiloids in certain rock layers in Tennessee.

Another type of fossil is called a trace fossil, which shows movement of an organism across soft mud, clay, or sand. Ancient trace fossil imprints, such as burrows and trails, were made as a creature scurried along a muddy riverbank in search of food, rested along the sandy seashore, or crawled along a beach to lay eggs—much like modern, crawling land or sea creatures. Trace fossils also include fossilized dung called coprolites. Coprolites of dinosaurs, fish, and other or-

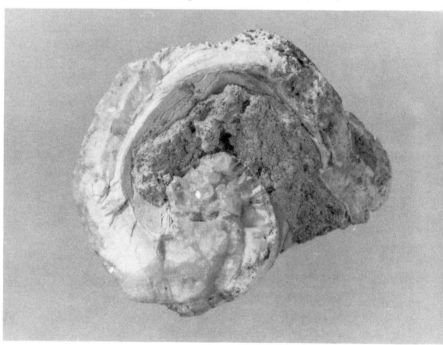

This spiral-shaped gastropod is close to three inches in diameter and its shell is replaced with the mineral calcite.

ganisms often contain the teeth and bones of what the predatory animal ate, and is direct evidence of the types of tiny organisms that lived in an area at that time.

Where Are Fossils Found?

There are three families of rock on the earth: sedimentary, igneous, and metamorphic. Sedimentary rock is preexisting rock that is deposited as soft sand, mud, silt, and clay as the result of the erosion (or wearing down) of rock. Fossils are usually found in sedimentary rock. The other rock types—igneous (rock formed from hot rock deep below the surface of the earth) and metamorphic (rock changed by heat and pressure)—are exposed to a great deal of geologic activity. Such movements, pressures, and heat can easily destroy fossils.

Large fossils of bones or other ancient organism remains can be found in many areas around the world. Most are found along highways and back roads in rock outcrops or in rock quarries. Others are often found in very strange places. Giant 3-foot (1-meter) Ammonites, sea creatures that lived in hard, spiral shells, are found in the stones that line the walls and doorway arches of many old homes in Lyme Regis, England. These homes, some more than 300 years old, were built from the local rock containing the ancient fossils.

Some fossil bones will never be found. Many have been eroded by wind and ice; or by the constant action of waves along the ocean coastlines or currents of rivers. In other areas, the fossils have been crushed by the movement of great mountain chains, or by the sudden shake of an earthquake. In fact, there may be some animal or plant species that will never be known—as there is no fossil record of the species within the rock layers.

Keeping Fossil Finds

Where in the world are fossils kept today? Most fossils are kept in famous museums. The Peabody Museum in New Haven, Connecticut, contains fossils of American dinosaurs and early mammals. The National Museum of Natural History at the Smithsonian Institution in

Washington, D.C., has fossils representing most of the phases of prehistoric life. The American Museum of Natural History in New York City is famous for its displays of mounted skeletons from around the world, including amphibians, reptiles, mammals, fossil eggs, and skin imprints. In fact, no other museum contains so many dinosaurs!

There are also major centers that revolve around local fossil finds. The Los Angeles County Museum of Natural History has the world's largest collection of fossil bones from a period ending around 10,000 years ago—most from the nearby La Brea tar pits. Dinosaur National Monument in Utah is the site of the Carnegie Quarry, where one can view scientists freeing thousands of dinosaur bones from the hard rock.

In Beijing (Peking), China, the Beijing Natural History Museum contains many of the Chinese dinosaur finds, including some of the largest in the world such as the *Shantungosaurus*. In England, places such as the Sedgwick Museum at Cambridge University display dinosaur fossils of local origin. The British Museum of Natural History in London contains more than three million fossils on display or in storage.

Some fossils are so prevalent in certain regions of the United States that states have adopted official fossils. For example, in 1984, the Alabama House of Representatives designated the ancient whale, *Basilosaurus cetoides*, as the Alabama fossil. The fossil was discovered in 1975 and is now on exhibit at the Red Mountain Museum in Birmingham.

2

Changes Over Time

The animal looked like any other horse on the prairie. Its nostrils flared as it smelled the approach of the thunderstorm. All around, wind and debris swirled around the animal, coating it with a fine layer of dust. Other horses cried out at a flash of lightning and the sudden sound of thunder. After running through a pass nearby, the horse found an overhanging rock just tall enough to hide under. After all, the ancestor of today's horse was about the size of a fox.

Fossil evidence shows that many species of organisms have changed drastically over time. In hundreds of millions of years, there have probably been more than a million different species to live on the earth. Shelled creatures have scurried across the ocean floor; dinosaurs have stalked smaller dinosaurs and amphibians along a river bank; and more recently, humans have walked on the earth. All this time, offspring of certain species evolved into different creatures, such as the change of fish to amphibians; while some animals died out all together, such as herds of giant elk that lived around 14,000 years ago.

If you look closely at the bones from various creatures, there seems to be a common thread. If you look from the wings of a bat to the fins of a whale to the hands of a human, it is often interesting to note the similarities. All of them have fingerlike bones that are used for grasping, hanging, or swimming. All of the bones represent the animals' long ancestries, or millions of years of change to fit their needs and environment.

Many organisms left behind bones and other hard parts, evidence for the scientists to form theories and conclusions about the changes in animals over time. But there are still many questions. Did larger-boned animals survive better than those with smaller bones? How and why did the various animals adapt and change their hard parts over time? And why did some creatures die out completely?

Scientists have spent years trying to answer such questions. Not all the answers have been found; and there are many different opinions. But all agree that little would be known about our ancient world if it were not for big bones and other fossil evidence.

Is Bigger Better?

Is bigger better when talking about bones? Is there some type of advantage to being large? Some of the largest bones, especially of dinosaurs, are over 10 feet (3 meters) in size! But many of these big boned animals have disappeared in a very short time. Does this prove that the creatures with the larger bones do not always have the advantage?

It may appear that large boned organisms have usually dominated the land and sea over time. But in certain periods, including today, smaller creatures were probably more numerous and produced more offspring. The idea that bigger is better may be due to the number of bones found. Larger bones are more resilient and can withstand millions of years of burial merely because they are larger. Smaller bones are more apt to be eroded, washed away, or dissolved in the rock. Larger bones are also easier to find than smaller bones. And finds of larger bones are reported on the news more than those of smaller bones.

Today, scientists are still studying whether or not bigger bones are better. One study is taking place in Africa on the Gombe chimps. Jane

Goodall, who has studied and described the Gombe chimps' social lives for over three decades, has also collected chimpanzee skeletons when members of the chimp study group die. By comparing the known development and medical history of the chimp, and knowing its bone structure, scientists hope to answer such questions as are bigger bones better? Do chimps with the larger bones seem to, along with their offspring, survive better than chimps with smaller bones? In addition, the study of chimp bones may tell why Gombe chimps have evolved smaller bodies than their ancestors.

Adapting by Wandering

The study of the movement of animals across the world over time is also important. It shows how creatures can move from place to place and adapt to changes in the environment around them—a very important factor in the change of bones and other hard parts over time.

How do scientists know animals have moved around the planet? In 1921, South African geologist A. L. Du Toit studied animal fossils on the various continents. In the late 1980s, the Dinosaur Project, an international study that includes many dinosaur sites, found evidence of similar creatures in different areas. These studies had one thing in common: the scientists who worked on the projects had found like fossils on separated continents—fossil evidence that these pieces of land were once joined. For example, the scientists who work on the Dinosaur Project have found that there was a link between the dinosaurs of northern Asia and North America.

How could these links have happened, especially since those land areas today are often separated by water? Paleontologists have tried to explain how fossils of similar species are found on different continents, often times separated by vast oceans, or between closer pieces of land. They reason that millions of years ago, the continents looked much different. Some areas that are dry today were once underwater; while regions that are underwater today were once dry.

The reason behind this change in the land is that the earth is never still. Its crust is broken into irregular plates that are in constant, slow motion all over the planet. Sometimes these movements cause the continents to appear to split into pieces or fuse together. Added to the earth's movements is the rise and fall of the oceans and the formation of great mountains. All these activities have often lead to drastic changes in the environment and often forced a species to move.

There may be other ways in which the different creatures have wandered from place to place. One idea is rafting, where the animal actually rides a branch or other piece of debris and travels across the

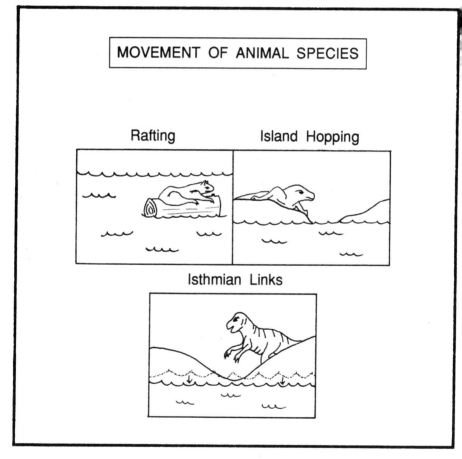

Animals often travel from place to place using these methods.

water. Another suggestion is that islands may have at one time acted as stepping stones, allowing creatures to swim the short distances from island to island. And still another idea points to links of land—called isthmian links—which may have appeared with the lowering of sea level, allowing the animals to cross into new territory. After thousands to millions of years, the land links disappeared with the rising of sea level.

Fossils show that because the land and sea have changed over time, so did the wandering of ancient animals. Dinosaurs that once roamed northern Asia had a land bridge to cross into northern North America. The land bridge did not last too long, probably less than a million years. But it was enough time for the dinosaurs to find new lands for food and territory.

There were also creatures that were not great travelers, staying in one region for millions of years. Two such groups are the Australian marsupials (such as the kangaroo) and monotremes (such as the duck-billed platypus). When these mammals arrived in Australia, they adapted by occupying vacant ecological niches and never left.

From One Species to Another

How did creatures, over time, adapt to fit the changing environment? The idea of offspring reflecting a change in a species is important. Changes in creatures around the world have always been controlled by the genes of the species. The study of heredity and the causes of variation in organisms is called genetics. Genes are the complex molecules within a cell that transmit specific characteristics from the parent to the offspring. Genes are the reason why children can look a great deal like their parents or even their grandparents.

Through time, changes in the genes of various species have often been brought on by a change in the environment. Such changes caused the creatures to split into another type of species, often changing their looks or hard parts. For example, the cotylosaurs—the first reptiles—gave rise to other types of reptiles, including the pelycosaurs. The pelycosaurs had differentiated teeth—including incisors, canines, and molar teeth—unlike most of the other reptiles of the time, which mainly had teeth all of the same size and shape. The hadrosaurs were bipedal dinosaurs that evolved from another type of dinosaur species. These creatures had gradually changed by developing a duck-billed skull for feeding on water plants.

Another example of one species changing into another is a type of marine turtle. When the sea became too crowded in their region of the world, some turtles went to the land. When the land became too

Some of the first creatures that adapted to flight were the insects, such as this giant Maganeura dragonfly with a wingspan of 28 inches (70 centimeters).

crowded, several of the turtles headed for the sea again. After a million years, this marine creature had adapted by changing its skeletal frame from fins to feet to fins, and changed into a different species from its cousins on land.

Sometimes a creature develops characteristics much like their ancestors. These apparent reversals are called atavisms. One of the most interesting examples is the horse. Most modern horses are born with a single hoof. Occasionally, one will be born with an extra two or three toes. This is somewhat similar to an ancestor of the horse, the *Hyracotherium*, which had four toes in front and three in back. The

Shelled brachiopods adapt well to conditions in the oceans and are some of the most prolific organisms on earth.

modern horses with extra toes are often called "throwbacks." But in reality, these atavisms are an example of how genetic changes can be retained in a species.

Fast or Slow?

How did these life pattern changes occur over time? Based on fossil evidence, some scientists believe that creatures changed gradually. They believe that the oceans, air, and land slowly and naturally changed over time. Oxygen in the atmosphere could have increased or decreased, the land uplifted around a great mountain range, and the salinity of the sea changed. But no matter what the change, it probably happened gradually over a long period of time.

A species can be greatly affected by such long-term changes. Currents in the ocean, the climate, and differences in the level of the land often take thousands of years to change. If the changes are slow, the creatures usually adapt by producing offspring that are genetically different, creating modifications in a skeleton or changes in a digestive system enabling them to eat new types of food. The strongest creatures better adapted to environmental changes would survive and their offspring would reflect the new changes while the poorly adapted creatures and their offspring would become extinct.

Other scientists believe that various species have changed abruptly over time. They believe that a sudden natural occurrence changed the conditions around the earth. Genetically, the creatures could not have changed in a short time. But such a quick change of the environment— a violent volcanic eruption that covers an area with dust or a sudden violent storm—can wipe out areas where organisms found a certain type of food. If a small number of a certain species lived in a very small area, the entire group of animals could be eliminated. Species of larger groups could survive more readily, because there is a greater chance that some of the creatures would survive.

Short-term changes in the environment are often difficult for a species to survive. Those that adapt to the new conditions survive;

while those that do not adapt die. For example, calcium in early oceans may have increased quickly over time, allowing the strongest creatures, such as fishes, to rapidly adapt by using the extra calcium to build stronger and larger skeletons. The dinosaurs may have been eliminated by a sudden impact of space objects on the earth. When the large creatures could not quickly adapt to the changes and died, the way was cleared for other smaller animals that survived the impacts.

Lost Through Extinction

Fossil bones may have shown us that there have been numerous adaptations to environmental conditions. But they also have shown that there have been countless extinctions of creatures over time. An extinction is when an entire species dies off, leaving only fossils as evidence of their existence. Extinctions seem to happen due to the inability of a creature to adapt to various conditions.

Many interesting mammals became extinct within the past 10,000 years. They were descendants of creatures that had gone through

Large rhinoceroses were known to roam parts of the earth, but became extinct a relatively short time ago.

millions of years of adaptations. Many of them were very large—including a 7.5-foot (2.3-meter) beaver called a *Castoroides*, and a 10-foot (3-meter) mammal armadillo called a *Glyptodon*. Today, there are very few large mammals. In the oceans, whales are largest; while on land, the elephant and hippopotamus are biggest. But where did the other larger mammals go? Why did they become extinct such a short time ago?

Scientists believe these extinctions occurred because of several reasons. One suggestion is that the climate and land changed. Around 200,000 years ago, an ice sheet covered parts of North America. After numerous advances and retreats, the giant ice sheet finally melted and retreated 10,000 years ago. Some scientists believe that the change in climate (from cold to warm) and the changes in land (with a great deal more water as the ice melted) caused animal territories and available food to change. Such major changes could have caused the extinction of the larger mammals. Another theory is that humans spread and took up territory, hunting the animals until they were no longer able to breed in large groups. But other scientists argue that there were too many mammals and too few humans to cause such an extinction.

What are some of the fossils found on the earth today? And what do they tell about the creatures that lived on the ancient earth? Some had adapted by building tough outer shells, and others supported their immense body by a thick internal skeleton. There have been millions of species of animals on this planet— sometimes leaving evidence for us in the form of fossils.

3

The First Steps

The scientific excursion was one of many studying the various organisms in the warm waters around Australia. Scientists on the excursion saw growths that looked almost like giant mushrooms. They may have looked strange, but the scientists knew that the funny shaped rocks held one of the oldest forms of sea life on the planet: algae. Another relative of an ancient organism was also found all around the scientists—in the air, on the land, and in the water—namely, bacteria. The tiny one-celled algae represent the forerunners of the first primitive plants; while bacteria are the descendants of the first creatures on the earth.

The oldest rocks found to date on earth are located in a frozen region of Canada and are around 3.96 billion years old. Fossil remains of bacteria and algae have been found only in much younger rock. One such fossil is a primitive form of bacteria called *Kakabekia*, a two-billion-year-old organism that resembles a very tiny umbrella with a long stalk. Another is *Aspergillus*, a mold or fungi that produces shoots as it grows. These are only two types of the oldest life known on the planet; there are several more. Scientists know they will find even more in the future as they search other ancient rocks on the earth.

These earliest organisms were the first to grow and spread around the earth's oceans. They had no hard parts, but left their impressions in the rock. Several of these organisms quickly adapted in different ways, and evolved into various types of multi-celled organisms. Those creatures that did survive as fossils have given scientists a good look at the ancient past.

The fossils leading up to organisms with larger and more complex bones are very important. They were the first steps toward creatures with hard parts; and because of a multitude of adaptations to the environment, they grew and diversified over millions of years. Each organism, no matter how small or large, was an important step in the natural history of the earth.

Burst of Growth

Around 600 million years ago, there was a burst of growth of multi-celled organisms in the oceans. The organisms on the earth at this time were mainly small, as evident in the fossils found in sedimentary rocks of this age. Not only were these creatures abundant, but there were also broad differences in size, shape, color, and habits between each type of organism. In addition, there was a lack of creatures with skeletons.

The earliest marine fossils show that something changed suddenly from the soft jellyfish and worms. In only 100 million years, animals appeared with scales and spines; and other creatures grew tubes and shells. These hard parts seemed to appear out of nowhere and were the forerunners to animals with skeletons.

Why did the animals suddenly develop hard parts? Some scientists believe that hard parts were needed for protection. Before hard shells or exteriors were common, predators could easily prey on other soft-bodied creatures. The hardened shells or spines made it more difficult for predators to get to the soft, internal organs of their prey. But more fossils need to be found to support this theory.

The best example of this new change were the trilobites, organisms that are only found today as fossils. Trilobites lived from around 600 to 250 million years ago, and were the first creatures known to have jointed legs—one segment for walking, and one for respiration. The trilobite also had an external skeleton, as hard as bone, that supported all of its soft organs. When threatened, the trilobite would curl up into a ball. Many fossil trilobites—which range in size from less than 1 inch (2.54 centimeters) to close to 18 inches (46 centimeters) in length—are often found in this curled position.

Fossils of brachiopods (meaning "arm foot") are the remains of small shelled creatures that evolved in the shallow marine waters around 600 million years ago. The rounded shells that cover the brachiopod's body differ in size and shape, and were made of part chitin—a plastic organic material. The brachiopods branched out into thousands of species over time. Today, around 200 species still exist. One small creature that evolved from the brachiopods is the *Lingula*, with a tongued-shaped shell and long wormlike body. Today the

Trilobites did not adapt to the changes in the environment and eventually became extinct.

Lingula lives in muddy sea bottoms just as it did 400 million years ago.

There are also numerous ancient fossils of creatures called bryozoans. These organisms, also called moss animals or sea mats, lived near shallow seas and grew by budding into colonies. There are over 4,600 species found as fossils, and 3,000 species live today. One of the strangest shaped bryozoans is the *Archimedes*, a spiral-shaped fossil around 350 million years old.

Creatures called graptolites left behind many hard fossils and impressions in sedimentary rock. Graptolites—small organisms that looked like thin twigs with serrated edges—were abundant around 500 million years ago, but became extinct around 355 million years ago. These strange-looking organisms are usually found as fossils in black

These spiral-shaped bryozoans lived some 345 million years ago, but their ancestors evolved around 400 million years ago in the shallow seas.

shale, a sedimentary rock that forms in water with poor bottom circulation. Their skeletons were chitinous rather than the usual shells and skeletons made of calcite.

Organisms called deposit feeders had hard parts and lived at the bottom of the ocean, feeding on smaller organic particles in the sediment. Similar to these organisms were the bottom dwellers, which attached themselves to the floor of the ocean or to the shells of some other organism such as a clam, and caught food as it floated by. Some tiny organisms were planktonic, passively floating or weakly swimming through the ocean waters. As time progressed, active swimming types of organisms—or nektonic organisms—emerged. All of these organisms either had few or no hard parts.

Fishes Find a Home

Around 500 million years ago, important creatures developed on the earth, both in the oceans and in freshwater: the first fishes. Fossil evidence shows that fishes probably evolved from echinoderms, a group that includes modern starfishes and sea urchins.

Along with the advent of fishes, skeletons became more complex. The first fishlike organisms were invertebrates (or organisms without a backbone). They were streamlined, almost like the shape of a baseball bat! These early fishes had elongated bodies and moved by contracting the trunk and tail muscles. This motion would send waves down the body of the fish, much like how the modern eel moves through the water. They were jawless, with no hinge to open and close their mouth; most ate through a small slit or opening under the tip of their snout and had to digest the food without chewing. One of the oldest jawless fish fossils was found in 1988—a 470-million-year-old fish from southern Bolivia, South America.

Fossil bones show that the first true fishes were also the first vertebrates, or organisms with a backbone. Some of these fishes were jawless; but another type adapted by developing hinged jaws. These cold-blooded, gill-breathing fishes moved through the oceans with a

27

side-to-side movement of their trunk and tail. One of the first jawed fishes were the acanthodians, which were scaly with large eyes and many small teeth.

Around 350 million years ago, the jawless fishes were becoming less common. They were at a great disadvantage, as they could only eat fine pieces of dead organisms on the ocean floor, while the hinged-jawed fish could catch and chew larger organisms. In addition, the competition for territory and food with the fishes with hinged jaws increased. Many of the jawless fish species disappeared; and today, only a few species remain.

Fishes have been one of the most successful class of organisms on the earth—outnumbering all other vertebrates twenty to one. They have always been one of the most flexible organisms on the planet, adapting to changes in the food chain and the environment. Fishes dart from rock to rock to avoid their predators and swim at rapid speeds to evade capture or catch their prey. Over the years, many bottom feeders have adapted by flattening themselves and changing color, blending

Rocks from around the Green River in Wyoming contain some of the best preserved fossil fishes known.

in with the ocean floor. Others have developed camouflage to look like the terrain in which they live. Some fishes protect themselves with brightly colored spines and spikes that are usually carriers of deadly poisons.

Today more than 23,000 species of fishes are known to exist. Modern fishes, including their shapes and bone structures, are not much different from ancient ones. This great number of species is the result of the various environments in which fishes live—including the deep or shallow waters of the oceans, lakes, rivers, and streams. For example, water pressure is enormous at great ocean depths. At depths of around 3 miles (4.8 kilometers), pressure may be as great as four tons per square inch! But fishes are still known to occupy these harsh places. In fact, many of the deep ocean fishes resemble ancient ones that lived millions of years ago.

Based on fossil bones found in rock, scientists know that there were numerous types of fishes that lived in the waters of the world. Most represent the two recent types of fishes: the cartilaginous (chondrichthyes) and bony (osteichthyes). The two major divisions of the chondrichthyes are the sharks and rays. The osteichthyes, the most numerous group of fishes, are broken into two groups by the nature of their paired fins: the ray-fin and lob-fin fishes. The most highly-developed of modern fishes, the teleosts, belong to the ray-fin fishes.

Fossil bone evidence shows that in a very short time, life was starting to become more diverse and abundant around the whole planet. By the time fishes and other smaller marine creatures became abundant, the bones show that there were other organisms growing in number. These creatures were not afraid to venture out of the water, an important step in the development of creatures—especially their bones—on land.

Heading for Land

Fossil evidence indicates that, millions of years ago, not all of the activity was going on in the seas. Around 425 million years ago,

These are the jaws of a fossil shark, *Carcharodon megalodon*, that lived in the oceans millions of years ago. Notice how large they are compared to the people in the photo.

ancient arthropods called eurypterids made tentative attempts to crawl on nearby beaches. These creatures may have been the first animals to set their fins upon the land. One of the largest eurypterid fossils ever found is 9 feet (2.7 meters) in length.

Why did creatures begin to move from the oceans to the land? One reason was the growth of the first land plants. Many creatures adapted to the change to land by beginning to eat vegetation on land. In addition, many of the small sea creatures were fighting for territory. On land, they could find an abundance of both food and territory.

For example, around 380 million years ago, small organisms occasionally lived on the lands near the water. Fossils of the *Trigonotarbid*—a precursor to the spider and a tiny creature that may have been the first land animal to have lived in the Americas—have been found entrapped in the curved tips of a plant called *Lecercqui complexa*, often found as a fossil in certain Devonian rocks of New York. The spider probably hid among the leaves of the plant, searching for food and hiding from predators. Other animal remains are also found in this rock, such as mites and centipedes. These creatures, too, may have hid and looked for food among the plants.

Fossils also show that larger creatures were about to make the land at least part of their territory. About 350 million years ago, several types of fishes had worked their way onto the land. These fishes had developed lungs and could gulp air. When the water in the pond where they were living became stagnant with little oxygen, these creatures would survive by using their newly developed lungs. If the water in the pond evaporated, the fish often used their lobe shaped fins to crawl to the next pool of water. The adaptation of the fins to walk on land came out of the necessity to survive, making these fish the ancestors of the next major step in land animals: the amphibians.

4

First on the Land

The creature, called an *Ichthyostega*, moved slowly from the ocean's edge to the sandy shore. The rain pelted the creature, but it did not matter. The *Ichthyostega* was looking for a secluded spot to lay its soft-shelled eggs. It looked like a fish with small stubby legs; and as it walked along the shore, it never strayed far from the water. But its movement was a very important part in the development of animals: its bones had allowed it to travel on land, making it one of the first true amphibians—the first creature to live between the water and the land.

Amphibians were direct descendants of the ocean fishes, mainly from a group called the rhipidistian fishes, and are thought to be ancestors of modern frogs, toads, salamanders, and newts. Fossil evidence shows that one of the largest groups of air-breathing, early amphibians were the labyrinthodonts, so named because of their labyrinthlike tooth structure. These creatures had limbs that were jointed fins and their heads and tails were fishlike. The *Seymouria*, which lived in an area we now call Texas, was a labyrinthodont.

The fishes-turned-amphibians did not make a conscious decision to walk on land. Some scientists believe that the climate and land changed, making the competition for food and territory greater. This forced the stronger animals to adapt to the new conditions. Those creatures that could not adapt died. How did the fishes develop the necessary bones and muscles to walk on land? Fossil bones of amphibians show that, as the hardier fishes had offspring, they produced young with sturdier and more refined muscles and bones that could hold their bodies out of water. With time—millions of years, in fact—sturdy fins developed into much needed legs.

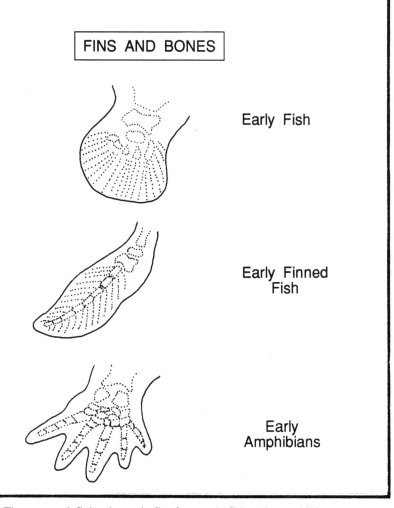

There was a definite change in fins from early fish to the amphibians.

Along with the changes of the amphibians' fins to legs, other muscular and bone structures changed to fit their movement to land. The creatures weighed more on land, causing them problems with body support. Amphibian skeletons had to become larger, with stronger bones in the legs and a better developed backbone.

Fossils also show that amphibians changed their methods of reproduction from those of fishes. They no longer laid unshelled eggs in the water, but eggs covered with a soft shell. The porous outer shell of the egg was able to "breathe," allowing a free flow of oxygen into the egg and to the growing amphibian. The porous shell also allowed the carbon dioxide that the young breathed out to escape from the egg and into the water. After hatching, the young breathed through gills, and were usually tadpole-shaped in their first few weeks of life.

In addition to structural changes, new adaptations in eating had to be developed. Food gathered on land is much different than food gathered in the water. Many of the new types of creatures were aquatic carnivores that fed on other fish. They had to learn new sources of food to survive, including other animals and plants along the shores.

The First Reptiles

Because of numerous adaptations on land, certain groups of amphibians started to lay special eggs. These eggs would hatch into young whose lungs could be used at birth. The shells were no longer soft, but hard and durable. These groups of amphibians had evolved into reptiles, the next step on land.

The reptiles were the first vertebrate group to raise their young on land—entirely independent of fresh or salt water. The tough shell of the egg was able to "breathe," allowing a free flow of oxygen into the egg and to the growing reptile. The egg was also a self-contained unit. Various membranes within the egg prevented liquids from escaping, and it contained food for the reptile (the yolk) as well as an area for the storage of wastes.

Reptiles spread rapidly throughout the land, searching for nesting sites and territory. Soon, because the reptiles adapted so well, they became true land animals, only approaching the water to drink and to search for food along riverbanks or ocean shorelines.

Fossil evidence shows that one of the first reptiles that may have given rise to many major reptile groups were the cotylosaurs. These primitive reptiles were small and mainly ate plants and insects. The cotylosaurs lived around the shores of rivers and oceans about around 280 million years ago, and they resembled modern turtles and tortoises.

Another group of reptiles that made their way onto the land at the same time were the pelycosaurs. These creatures were not timid, but were aggressive meat eaters, often with razor-sharp teeth to rip apart their food. One such reptile was the *Dimetrodon*, a 12-foot (3.6-meter) creature with a long pointed tail and a large fan on its back.

The true reptile family is divided into four groups, based on the pattern of openings in the back of their fossil skulls. There are the earliest reptiles called the anapsids, a group that probably includes today's turtles and tortoises. The synapsids were the mammal-like reptiles that lead to today's mammals. The diapsids were one of the largest groups of reptiles that included the dinosaurs, thecodonts, and mosasaurs. Today's lizards, snakes, birds and crocodiles are all members of this group. Lastly, the euryapsids were all marine reptiles, including the plesiosaurs and ichthyosaurs, and was a group that soon became extinct.

Bones of the various early reptiles have been found in many regions of the world, evidence that the creatures spread rapidly and covered many territories. But could reptiles have lived earlier than around 250 million years ago? One important find was in a quarry in Scotland in 1989. In a rock layer called the East Kirkton limestone, researchers found a 338-million-year-old reptile skeleton around 8 inches (20 centimeters) long, with a fossil skull more similar to a reptile than to an amphibian. When more of these fossils are found,

35

we may be able to better understand the evolutionary link between the amphibian and the reptile families.

Reptiles of the Sea

Not only were reptiles growing in number on land, but fossil finds also show that reptiles were becoming more abundant in the oceans. Some reptiles actually returned to the sea from the land; others had never ventured on land, always living in the water.

The reptiles that returned to the sea readapted to the water environment, their feet gradually evolving again into flippers. They also adapted other physical features to make swimming in the ocean much faster and more efficient. When these marine reptiles returned to the sea, they found that the vast oceans offered more territory and food than on land. Most of them did not return to the land to lay their eggs, but adapted to the water environment to reproduce.

One of the first reptiles to head back to the oceans was the ancestor to today's turtles, found as fossils in 250-million-year-old rock. Some turtles did stay between the land and the water, and are the ancestors of the modern box turtle; but other turtles headed for the water. By around 60 million years ago, these turtles adapted to the oceans and grew to sizes of 8 to 12 (2.4 to 3.7 meters) feet and weights of 1,200 to 3,000 pounds (540 to 1,400 kilograms), as the water easily supported their great bulk.

Reptiles that remained in the sea were also evolving. One group, the mosasaurs—ancestors of some modern lizards—were prevalent in the early oceans, and grew up to 26 feet (8 meters) in length. They resembled today's lizards, but had four flipperlike limbs, different teeth, and a long, flat tail that they used for propulsion. Mosasaur fossils show that they were predators, feeding on the abundant fish in the earth's oceans. The broken bones of jaws, skulls, and vertebrae near these fossils also show that these creatures were fierce fighters—not only with other ocean organisms, but with each other.

The euryapsids were a major group of marine reptiles. One

member of this group, the placodonts, invaded the seas around 200 million years ago. These reptiles had short, stout bodies with bony armor, and feet with webbing between the toes. The placodonts became skilled in eating shellfish by ripping the shells from the ocean bottom. Fossils of these reptiles are not found in rock past 195 million years old, as other ocean creatures eventually outfought the placodonts for territory and food.

Fossil evidence shows that reptiles larger than the mosasaurs and euryapsids also invaded the oceans. One such group was the plesiosaurs, barrel-shaped creatures often reaching up to 33 feet (10 meters) in length. These large reptiles were good hunters and swimmers. They had a small head on a long neck, and used their strong limbs for powerful strokes in the water. They would often stretch their long necks and snake their heads through the water, catching their food with their needle-sharp teeth.

The ichthyosaurs were reptiles that were best adapted to ocean life.

Fossils also show that some marine reptiles resembled modern creatures. Ichthyosaurs, or fish-lizards, were reptiles that adapted best to ocean life. They were streamlined, with limbs that resembled the fins of modern dolphins. The tail of the ichthyosaurs changed over the reptiles' years in the oceans, becoming more efficient for propulsion. Based on the fossil animals in many ichthyosaurs' stomachs and fossil droppings, the creatures fed mainly on fish, shellfish, and eventually, cephalopods.

The First to Fly

The first large flying creatures were ancestors of reptiles. But fossils of smaller flying creatures have been found in great abundance in older rock. One of the oldest groups is the flying insects. The first insects, around 410 million years ago, were wingless; but around 100 million years later, wings were the major features of cockroaches and the ancestors of the dragonfly. By 280 million years ago, fossil evidence shows that more advanced insects grew in abundance all over the earth, and are still seen in great numbers today.

From fossil evidence, scientists believe that, by around 180 million years ago, certain reptiles had to learn how to fly in their search for food and new territory. Called pterosaurs, these flying creatures had either short or long tails, long pointed beaks, fingers on the top of the wing (much like the modern bat) and wide wing spans. Scientists believe that these reptiles could not really fly, mainly because of their skin-covered wings, but glided from tree to tree or from a tree to the ground. The smallest pterosaurs were sparrow-sized; while, one of the largest pterosaur fossils had a wing span of 50 feet (15 meters)—equivalent in size to a small aircraft! One large pterosaur fossil was found at Big Bend National Park in Texas and was named the *Quetzalcoatlus*, or "feathered serpent," after an Aztec god.

Flying reptiles were eventually replaced by a new creature in the skies—the ancestors of the birds. Fossil evidence shows that birds began to dominate because of two major adaptations. First, the birds could tuck their wings into their bodies and easily move about on the ground, ready to fly at a moment's notice of trouble. Second, unlike the pterosaurs' skin-covered wings, the birds' wings were covered with feathers, which were lightweight and easy to move and separate.

The oldest known bird is the *Archaeopteryx*, a crow-sized creature that lived around 150 million years ago. Fossils of the bird's bones show that the creature walked like a crow, but could not sustain long

This pterosaur was one of the first real large flying creatures.

periods of flight. Around five skeletons and one feather imprint have been found in sedimentary rock in Germany. The bird looks a great deal like a reptile—with teeth in the upper and lower jaws, fingers in the forewings, and a long tail made of feathers and bone vertebrae. Though controversy still surrounds the fossils of the delicate imprints of forelimb feathers, the *Archaeopteryx*, it is still the major candidate for being the first bird.

Fossils show that other flying creatures soon followed, many adapting to the oceans. One, the *Hesperornis*, was a diving bird that could not fly or walk, but could swim very well. Strong flight muscles were developed in the *Ichthyornis*, an ocean bird that resembled a stout, modern tern. Land birds soon became abundant, especially shorebirds, songbirds, raptors, and owls.

Bones of long ago birds also show that flightless creatures evolved, having birdlike characteristics, but adapting to life on the ground or along the rock in a cliff. The heaviest flightless bird known was the *Aepyornis maximus* (or "greatest of the high birds"), which weighed close to 970 pounds (440 kilograms). The tallest flightless birds known were the *Dinornis giganteus*, measuring close to 11.5 feet (3.5 meters) in height. This species may have died out only 400 years ago! Today the Falkland Islands, an isolated archipelago of more than 700 islands located in the sub-Antarctic, is home to millions of the descendants of one of the oldest flightless avian groups to have lived on the earth: the penguin.

5

Growth on the Land

Bones found in the 200,000 acres of today's Dinosaur National Monument in Utah are some of the best in the world. Over the years, since the fossil field was found, it has yielded heads, hip bones, teeth, and other skeletal parts. The bones are not like those of today's creatures. They are much larger and heavier. They are the bones of the greatest land creatures that ever lived: the dinosaurs.

It is difficult to imagine creatures that were taller than a two-story house, with leg bones taller than the average human. Yet, during the reign of the dinosaurs, there were several very tall reptiles, including the *Tyrannosaurus rex* , at 39 feet (12 meters) in length and 18.5 feet (5.6 meters) in height; or the *Diplodocus*, a dinosaur that measured 87 feet (26.5 meters) in length!

Evidence of dinosaurs in the form of fossils has been found in numerous places all over the earth. Some dinosaur bone fields have yielded well-preserved fossils. Other bones are small and in pieces, broken by predators that ate the creatures after a fight, or fractured through exposure to wind, water, and ice over time. But many are superb examples of the creatures that once roamed and dominated the land for 140 million years.

The First Dinosaurs

Many of the biggest fossil bones and teeth have come from dinosaurs, since these creatures included some of the largest land creatures ever. Dinosaurs also came in all sizes and shapes, including those that ran on two feet or four; those that ate flesh or plants; and those that ranged from the size of a chicken to close to 100 feet (30 meters) in length.

Fossils show that a major step towards the dinosaurs was a group of reptiles called the thecodonts. They were larger and faster than many other reptiles, and had adapted to changes in food and territory by becoming meat eaters instead of insect and plant eaters. Not only did the thecodonts give rise to the dinosaurs, but also to the pterosaurs and crocodiles—all grouped as archosaurs, or the "ruling reptiles."

The true dinosaurs were one of the most successful creatures to have roamed the earth, and lived until around 65 million years ago. They are divided into two major groups: the ornithischians and the

This dinosaur dig has been working since the early 1900's, with many finds still taking place today.

saurischians. Dinosaurs dominated the lands and were fierce in protecting their territories and their young. During this time, smaller, mammal-like creatures also began to spread, but they tried to stay away from the much larger predatory dinosaurs by hiding in trees or small holes and by looking for food under the cover of night.

Dinosaur Fossils

Like the creatures themselves, dinosaur fossils come in many shapes and sizes. Also, because the reptiles were so large, their bones are large. It did not matter if the dinosaur was a carnivore or a herbivore; both types of fossil bones are still very large.

There are also other fossils associated with the dinosaurs, not just bones. There are footprints, skin imprints, teeth, and occasionally, dinosaur eggs. Like bones of the ancient dinosaurs, such features as the footprints of dinosaurs tell a great deal about the creatures. For example, by studying the footprints of the giant plant eaters, scientists

This fossilized tree branch was part of a tree during the dinosaur reign.

believe that the great animals were not clumsy and slow, as first thought. The prints show, based on the distance between the animals' strides, that some dinosaurs were quick and active. Apparently, carnivorous dinosaurs moved faster, around 10 miles (16 kilometers) an hour, compared to the herbivores, which traveled around 5 miles (8 kilometers) an hour.

Egg fossils also show a great deal about the different types of nesting habits of the dinosaurs. One such nest of fossil dinosaur eggs was found in 1923, in Outer Mongolia's Gobi Desert. The eggs in this nest were elongated, 8 inches (20 centimeters) in length, and were probably from the horned dinosaur called the *Protoceratops*. The nests carried up to thirty eggs—too many for one dinosaur to lay. These nests show that this dinosaur, and probably others, followed a regular social pattern, and laid their eggs in a communal nest.

The dinosaur egg shells were highly porous, and the surface was covered with ridges, wrinkles, or bumps. Most of the shells were relatively the same size because if one egg were any larger, the egg shell would have to be thicker. And if the shell were thicker, it would not allow the egg to "breathe" out oxygen and release carbon dioxide.

After the dinosaur laid the eggs, it would cover the clutch of eggs with sand, warming the eggs and allowing the young to hatch on their own. The embryo inside each egg often reached a size of around 10 to 12 inches (25 to 30 centimeters) before it would break its way through the shell.

One of the oldest fossil eggs was found in Texas. Other regions yield shell fragments, and occasionally, whole eggs. Fossil eggs from Provence, many measuring up to 9.8 inches (25 centimeters), are believed to be from a *Hypselosaurus*.

The End of the Giants

Around 65 million years ago something strange happened: the dinosaurs became extinct. The fossil record shows that around fifty percent of all other organisms on the earth—small and large creatures from the oceans, the air, and on land—also became extinct at this time.

There had already been extinctions of other smaller species over time, such as the trilobites. Fossils of these extinct species have shown that the creatures died out because of competition for food and territory with other animals. But there have never been extinctions of creatures as big as the dinosaurs, and the cause is not clear.

What caused the demise of all these large boned creatures? There are numerous theories or ideas. One theory is that a faraway star exploded, sending dust and gas that eventually hit the earth. Another theory states that a huge space object (or several space objects) bombarded the earth around 65 million years ago, sending debris and dust high into the air that eventually cut off the sunlight. Still another theory states that the dinosaurs died because of a biological catastrophe. For example, a disease that destroyed bone tissue could have affected certain animal species, but not affected others.

More Recent Mammals

According to the fossil record, and recent observation, one group of organisms seemed to do quite well during and after the time of the dinosaur extinction: the mammals. It appears that after the larger animals died off, the mammals began to find new, unclaimed territory. This allowed the animals to spread rapidly throughout the land, leading to one of the most successful types of creatures on earth today. Other smaller creatures also survived with the mammals, including numerous species of insects, snakes, crocodiles, lizards, turtles, and birds. It was fortunate that mammals could eat the insects and plants that survived after the dinosaur extinction. Otherwise, without food, many of the mammals would also have become extinct.

How are mammals different than other animal groups? Mammals are warm-blooded, with better body temperature controls to adapt to changes from hot to cold. Whereas most reptiles are cold-blooded and need the warmth of the sun to keep their bodies active. Mammals are also covered with fur or hair, unlike the scales of the reptiles. And mammals give birth to live babies and they nurse their young; they do not lay eggs like amphibians and reptiles.

In the early 1900s, American paleontologist Henry Fairfield Osborn noted fossils may indicate that the first mammals originated within the continent of Asia, but no one knows for sure. What fossils do show is that mammals have been the most successful creatures to live on the earth in the past several million years. They are the direct descendants of the reptiles from a group called the pelycosaurs and other mammal-like reptiles. One of the reasons that scientists believe these reptiles are ancestors of the mammals is because of the animals' fossil bones: openings in the skull changed from the reptiles to the mammal.

One of the earliest known true mammal fossils belongs to the *Megazostrondon*, or "big girdled tooth." This tiny creature probably

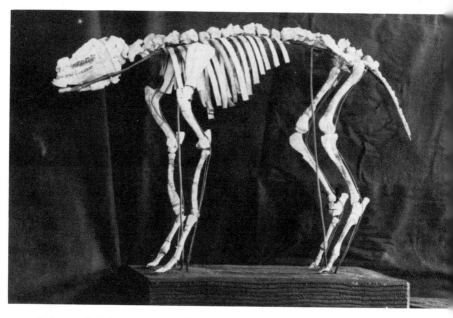

This camel skeleton was around more than 10,000 years ago and is the ancestor of the modern camel.

suckled its young on milk, based on the fossil teeth found. And unlike reptiles that had continuously replaced teeth, this mammal had a permanent set of teeth. Like many of the early mammals, the *Megazostrondon* hunted for its food of insects at night, preferring to remain out of sight from the larger predators.

Fossils show that, though the predatory dinosaurs were gone, there were other creatures that fed upon mammals. One was the *Diatryma*, a bird that could chase down smaller mammals. The bird was flightless, but could run at very high speeds. And it could pull apart its prey with its sharp parrotlike beak.

For 20 million years, the *Diatryma* chased down mammals; but they did not eradicate the mammals. In fact, mammals were beginning to take over as the dominant group. Some mammals were beginning to grow in size, such as the *Diprotodon*, a large ancestor of modern marsupials, which measured around 11 feet (3.4 meters) in length. And ancestors of the horse, deer, sheep, giraffe, and hippopotamus were also starting to grow in numbers.

Ancient horses' teeth are often found around Myrtle Beach, South Carolina, and are over a million years old.

Fossil evidence shows that mammals were beginning to grow in size and number in the oceans as well. Scientists believe that the ancestors of ocean mammals appeared as far back as 50 million years ago.

Some creatures lived on the land until the competition for territory forced many of them to the oceans. Ancestors of the whales, dolphins, and porpoises (also called cetaceans) were such creatures, and are descendants of a land animal related to the horse and other hoofed mammals. One of these groups was the mesonychids, including the *Basilosaurus*, a fierce, carnivorous creature that lived in the oceans 50 million years ago.

Cetaceans rapidly adapted to the marine lifestyle, becoming hairless and streamlined. They no longer needed legs, so they adapted by developing fins; while their feet evolved into horizontal tail flukes needed for propulsion in the seas. Cetaceans also became larger, easily held by the buoyancy of water.

Human Fossils

Human bones probably show some of the best adaptations of any organism on the earth. Bones have a great deal to do with the success of the human species. About three to four million years ago, humanlike animals began to roam the plains and highland areas. Groups of these animals began to walk upright, giving them a chance to see greater distances. Just notice how a grizzly bear will stand upright to smell the wind for food or an enemy nearby. But, unlike the bear, the humanlike animals adapted by staying on their feet. Ancestors of modern humans were the first successful bipedal mammals; while other mammals remained on all four legs. Even animals that resemble humans, such as the ape or the chimpanzee, walk on four legs.

Humans are considered primates, a group that includes monkeys, apes, and lemurs. And though humans are considered to be one of the most intelligent and adaptable of any other animal species, it was the change of their skeleton that helped them to survive. One of the main reasons for humans' ability to walk upright was because of how their skeleton evolved. Bones changed to meet the needs of finding food, hunting, running from predators, and eventually, making tools with which to live. And it is the development of the human bones over time that allowed humans to spread over the lands.

Bones that give scientists evidence of human adaptations come from ancient skeletons whose structures look like human bones. One major find was the skeleton scientists named Lucy. Her fossil bones were found in modern Africa. The scientific name for Lucy is *Australopithecus afarensis*, and she is considered a hominid, or a primate in the human family. Why do scientists believe Lucy is much like modern humans? Because of the way Lucy's hip bones are shaped, scientists can tell that she walked upright—one of the first steps towards *Homo sapiens*, or modern humans.

Other bones have changed over time, giving way to humans. The way the bones lie and grow in a human foot are much different than those in Lucy or an ape. The toes of the ape are shaped to allow the animal to hang from a tree. The bones in Lucy's foot allowed her to walk instead of climb. And recent human foot bones are balanced to make walking an easy task.

The bones in the human hand, especially the thumb, also developed over time—allowing humans to easily grasp objects. Because humans have an opposable thumb, they are able to grip objects better than other animals. Thanks to this adaptation, humans were able to develop and use various tools for hunting, food preparation, and building shelter.

The bones in the skull of humans have also changed. During Lucy's time, the jaw jutted out and the brain casing was more oval and flat. Hundreds of thousands of years later, the skull became larger and more rounded; and around one million years ago, the skull became larger, higher, and more rounded to hold a bigger brain. Modern humans (*Homo sapiens*) have a skull that holds a brain three times larger than other mammals their size.

There have been no perceived changes in human bones for around one million years. However, humans did change their outside appearance, based on the area and environment in which they lived. Witness the various continents around the world, and the variations in the skin color, features, and behavior of the people who live there. Each human appears to be different, and that is what makes the world exciting; but each human's bones have remained relatively the same.

Will human bones ever change? Will they become smaller or stronger? Since humans no longer hunt for food, search for shelter, or hide and run from predators, it is possible that their bones will not change significantly. Some scientists believe that if any changes do take place, it would have to be after many millions of years! But there are other fossil bones that need to be found so scientists can tell more about the early life of humans on earth.

Arrowheads are found in many sites where North American natives once lived—an indication of how humans developed tools with which to survive.

6

Famous Fossils and Fakes

It took many years before scientists realized the value of fossils. It took even more years before fossils were known to be the records of the earth's long history. Fossils were thought to be from living organisms as far back as the mid-1500s; but there was never a clear connection between them and history. Many people believed that the fossils had grown from seeds that grew in the rock! By 1667, Nicolas Steno, an Italian scientist, suggested that fossils were organic in nature. The next year, Robert Hooke, an English scientist, noted that animal-like fossils were actually the remains of ancient animals.

The real push in fossil discovery and interpretation occurred in the nineteenth century. In 1815, William Smith, "the father of geology," identified sedimentary rock layers by their fossils. Alexandre Brongniart was a nineteenth century geologist who also used fossils to name and date rock layers. The famous British naturalist, Charles Darwin, collected fossils while voyaging on the ship *H.M.S. Beagle* in the nineteenth century. These fossils helped him to develop his theory of evolution. Early collectors also included a young girl named Mary Anning who, in 1812—at the age of 12—unearthed Britain's first ichthyosaur, a relative of the dinosaur. She later became one of the most famous female "fossilists" of her time.

During the nineteenth century, in the United States, just after the Civil War, fossil finds were discovered—mainly of dinosaur bones. Two rival scientists, Othniel Charles Marsh and Edward Drinker Cope, were both determined to be the first to have a dinosaur collection. Cope explored Montana in 1876; while Marsh ventured into western Kansas and Colorado. For more than two decades, the scientists worked in secrecy, trying to beat each other in finds and ideas on dinosaurs. But even though neither scientist "won," several museums around the United States did—by receiving both scientists' collections. Some of the world's best fossil dinosaurs and other species are found in these samples.

Over time, some fossils have been found, but then lost. In 1847, at the top of Mt. Holly, Vermont, two tusks, a tooth, and some bones of an American mammoth (*Elephas primogenius*) were found by workers excavating a track bed for the Rutland Railroad. The mammoth, close to 10,000 years old, had been preserved in a deep basin much like a bog. Today, only the tooth and tusk remain because the bones deteriorated after being exposed to air!

As scientists became aware of the earth's many fossils, collections were started all over the world. Many have increased over the years, and scientists now know much more about the earth's past animals. And thanks to the numerous whole fossil bones of animals, scientists have been able to reconstruct various animals from these finds.

These ichthyosaur bones of a female adult show complex bones. The ichthyosaurs were one of the first dinosaur bones found.

Fossils in Tar and Ice

Most fossils are found in rock layers, but in one special place, the fossils are not found in rock. The La Brea tar pits near Los Angeles, California, contain numerous complete skeletons!

Around 14,000 years ago, large asphalt pits formed in this region, looking strangely like pools of water. As large and small animals and birds came to the pits, they discovered that the water was not water at all, and they became trapped in the thick, black tar. Unable to get out, they cried and struggled. Other predators heard the cries and came to investigate, and perhaps, to have an easy meal. But as they approached the helpless creatures, they, too, became caught in the tar. Most of the meat-eating creatures caught were often diseased, young, or injured. This may mean that the predators had a hard time catching food, and attacked the helpless creatures because they could not catch more active animals.

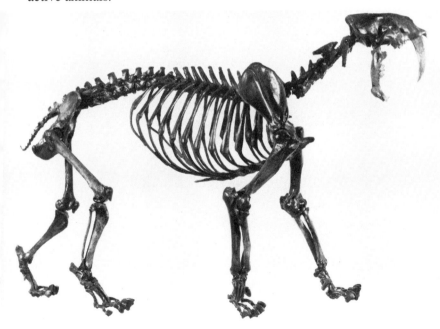

This skeleton of a saber-toothed cat was found in the tar pits of La Brea, near Los Angeles.

The asphalt pits at La Brea have been one of the most fertile fossil sites of more recent animals and birds. The pits formed from rock layers that contain oil and gas, forming pools of tar that turned to asphalt by exposure to air. The list of La Brea fossils is long, including animals such as horses, camels, bison, saber-toothed tigers, short-faced bear, black bear, skunks, weasels, badgers, mice, ground squirrels, the American mastodon, the Imperial mammoth, and ground sloths. Birds include hawks, turkeys, owls, pigeons, ravens, waterfowls, and others.

La Brea is not the only place where fossils are found in relatively good shape. There have also been rather ancient animal fossils, and sometimes whole animals, found in ice. In Siberia in 1976, prospectors in search of gold along the Kolyma River found a baby mammoth—a 17,000-year-old ancestor of today's elephant—frozen whole in the ice. The ice had caused the mammoth's softer parts to remain, stopping the decay that would have turned the creature into a fossil.

Is This a Bird?

Fossils of the oldest known bird come from a layer of limestone rock. The *Archaeopteryx*, was the first reptile known to have feathers, the precursor to today's songbirds and other feathered species. A number of fossils has shown that the *Archaeopteryx* was one of the first birds. But fossils of this bird have also created a great controversy in the scientific community.

Around 1859, the first discovery of the fossil skeleton of a birdlike creature was made in a quarry in southern Germany. The rocks were very fine grained, leaving only the bones of the specimen. In 1861, another creature was found, but besides the bones, fine detailed impressions of the bird's feathers were surrounding the skeleton. The fossil was named *Archaeopteryx lithographica*, or "ancient wing from lithographic limestone." (A lithograph was the closest to a photographic print at that time.) An even better fossil of the bird was

RESTORATION

FOSSIL

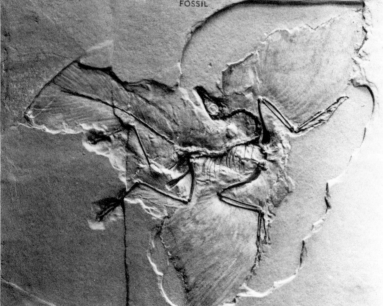

The *Archaeopteryx* was a crow-sized animal that may have been the first bird. Below, is the fossil evidence showing what are thought to be feathers, and above is an artist's rendition of what this animal may have looked like.

found in 1877, in the same area. It took until 1956 to find another fossil specimen, and three more since that time.

The controversy started early: several researchers believed that the delicate feather impressions were printed on the specimen. They claimed that feather impressions with such detail could not have survived and left an imprint on the rock. To add to the controversy, one fossil did not show any evidence of feathers surrounding the bird's skeleton. There is still controversy surrounding the fossils, with many scientists believing that the feather impressions are fake.

The bird fossils have also caused another controversy: where did the bird originate? Without feathers, the *Archaeopteryx* looks like a reptile. The first specimen that was found in 1859, was displayed in a Dutch museum for over 100 years, labeled as a pterosaur. But even today, scientists still argue as to the real origins of the first bird. Are birds relatives of the ornithischian dinosaurs? Are they relatives of the crocodiles? Or could they be related to the theropods? More fossils of the birds need to be found in order to resolve these problems.

The Cardiff Giant

There have always been fake fossil remains in the scientific world. But in the world of false fossils, one story stands out: the Cardiff Giant—once thought to be the ancient remains of a human giant.

The story of the giant starts with George Hull, a cigar manufacturer from Binghamton, New York. Taking a large block of gypsum rock from a quarry in Fort Dodge, Iowa, Hull had two marble cutters sculpt the slab into the likeness of a man measuring around 10 feet (3 meters) in height. In order to make the giant look ancient, Hull chipped off the statue's hair and some of the beard, two soft parts that would not have survived. He also hammered the statue with nails and dumped a gallon of sulfuric acid over the sculpture to make it look more aged and weathered!

In October, 1869, while workers dug a well on a farm near Cardiff, New York, the giant was uncovered. The "ancient" man was a great

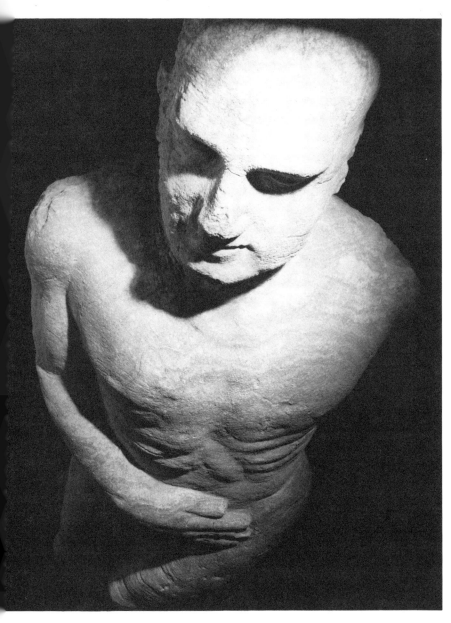

The Cardiff Giant was once thought to be the remains of a very ancient giant human.

success. As the "petrified" man was exhibited in many places across the state, there were debates among those who believed that the giant was the remains of an ancient wondrous race, and those who—especially geologists and paleontologists—could not believe such a fossil would survive, let alone turn into gypsum rock and end up in a tiny town in New York. By December, three months after the discovery, the two sculptors confessed that they had carved the statue. The hoax was over, but not before the whole country knew about the giant. Even today, the giant rock statue is a popular tourist attraction kept on display at the Farmer's Museum in Cooperstown, New York.

The Impossible Piltdown

Human bones were again the subject of an extraordinary find along the southeast coast of England in a town called Piltdown. Charles Dawson, who enjoyed hunting for fossils, had found a fragment of a skull in 1908, recovered after workers told him that they had unearthed and smashed a "coconut" in a nearby gravel pit. Dawson had become friends with French Jesuit priest and paleontologist Pierre Teilhard de Chardin, who felt Dawson's find of skull fragments were really the remains of a human, perhaps the link to modern humans.

After Dawson collected a few more fragments of the skull and a few other mammal fossils, he brought the pieces to Arthur Smith Woodward, a paleontologist at the British Museum, in 1912. Woodward, Dawson, and Teilhard went to the excavation at Piltdown, finding a jaw with its two molar teeth, including human patterns of wear on the ancient teeth. In December of that year, Woodward published a paper on the subject and the controversy began.

The apelike jaw in connection with the humanlike skull pieces raised interest in the scientific community. Could this be the missing link between apes and modern humans? It appeared to be; and in 1915, Dawson found a fragment of the right side of a skull at Piltdown 2, a site two miles (three kilometers) from Piltdown. Another lower molar worn down in a human fashion was found in the same year.

For around forty years, the idea of the Piltdown creature was debated. Were the fossils evidence of an ancient humanlike creature or not? In 1953, with Teilhard the only one of the trio still surviving, the truth came out: the Piltdown fossil pieces were fake. According to Kenneth Oakley, J. S. Weiner, and W. E. le Gros Clark, the Piltdown bones had been chemically stained to imitate aging, and the teeth filed down to simulate human wear. The pieces of flint that were supposedly carved by the ancient humans were recently made. Finally, the mammal bones were brought from another part of the country. The skull bones, amazingly, were from a modern human and the jaw, from an orangutan.

No one really knows who is responsible for starting the Piltdown forgery. Many think Dawson started the idea, and Teilhard—though he may have known about the fake bones—continued the controversy. There is no way to know the truth. But the incident is, again, a good example of how difficult it is to tell a true fossil from a fake one— especially when scientists really want to find the important fossils that link humans to their past.

Fossils have been invaluable to scientists studying the ancient creatures of the earth. And there are still many earth rocks to explore and more fossils to find. One day there may be fossil bones found of a creature that has never before been seen. Future fossils may be faked again; but, hopefully, scientists will have more sophisticated tools with which to analyze fossils. Whatever true fossils are found, no doubt they will be exciting. And no doubt they will bring people that much closer to finding out about their ancient past.

Glossary

algae—A variety of simple plants that may have been the first single-celled groups to develop on the earth.

ammonites—An extinct group of organisms common during the Mesozoic era whose shell resembles modern nautiloids.

amphibians—An organism that lives between the water and the land; laying its eggs in the water, and breathing with gills when it is young.

archaeologist—A scientist who studies ancient human remains.

atavism—The appearance of a physical characteristic typical of a distant ancestor in an organism.

bipedal—An organism that walks on two legs.

birds—A feathered vertebrate evolved from reptiles whose front legs have developed into wings.

bone—The hard parts of a vertebrate's skeleton.

brachiopods—A marine organism with two shells surrounding its soft internal organs.

carnivores—A meat-eating animal.

cast—A mold that becomes filled with a mineral or mud.

coprolites—Fossil dung of animals.

deposit feeder—An organism that feeds on sediments at the bottom of oceans, lakes, or streams.

dinosaurs—Two groups (ornithischians and saurischians) of reptiles that lived between 230 and 65 million years ago.

extinction—Any process that causes a species to die out completely.

fauna—A term for animals on the earth.

fishes—A vertebrate group that developed and spread widely in the oceans over time, having jaws, fins, and a tail.

flora—A term for plants on the earth.

food chain—An arrangement in which each creature is a link in the food cycle, feeding on other creatures below it in the hierarchy.

fossils—Any remains or traces of an organism; fossils are usually found in sedimentary rock, but can also be preserved in ice or tar.

genetics—The study of heredity and the interactions of genes producing similarities and differences between organisms.

geologic time scale—A scale that represents the different divisions of time, from the birth of the earth to the present day.

herbivore—A plant-eating organism.

ichnologist—A scientist who studies the footprints of various animals.

igneous rock—A group of rocks formed from molten material.

invertebrate—An animal without a backbone.

isthmian links—Narrow strips of land connecting two larger landmasses allowing organisms to move from one place to another.

mammal—A vertebrate with four limbs. It is warm blooded, and often covered with hair or fur; females produce young and milk from special glands.

metamorphic rock—A group of rocks formed from preexisting rock that has been changed, especially by heat and pressure.

mold—An impression of an organism left after a fossil in a rock is dissolved away.

organism—Any living thing, including plants and animals.

ornithischians—A major group of dinosaurs (including the *Stegosaurus*) whose hips resemble those of birds.

paleontologist—A scientist who studies ancient life, especially using fossil evidence.

primates—An order of mammals including humans, apes, and lemurs.

quadruped—An organism that walks on four legs.

reptiles—A vertebrate with dry, scaly skin; often cold blooded and lays its eggs on land.

saurischians—A major group of dinosaurs (including *Tyrannosaurus rex*) whose hips resemble those of lizards.

sedimentary rock—Rock formed from the deposit of sediments that harden over time; fossils are found in sedimentary rock.

species—A certain group of living things that can only reproduce among themselves.

thecodonts—Reptiles that were the ancestors of the dinosaurs.

trace fossil—A fossil that represents tracks of animals.

trilobites—An extinct animal with the first known efficient eyes.

vertebrate—An animal with a backbone.

Further Reading

Barnes-Svarney, Patricia L. *Clocks in the Rocks: Learning About Earth's Past.* Hillside, N.J.: Enslow Publishers, 1990.

Bower, Bruce. "Biographies Etched in Bone," *Science News* (August 18, 1990). pp. 106-108.

Cole, Joanna. *The Human Body: How We Evolved.* New York: William Morrow & Company, Inc., 1987.

Fenton, Carroll Lane. *Tales Told by Fossils.* New York: Doubleday & Company, Inc., 1966.

Gould, Stephen, J. *Hen's Teeth and Horse's Toes.* New York: W. W. Norton & Company, 1984.

Lambert, David. *The Field Guide to Prehistoric Life.* New York: Facts on File Publications, 1985.

Lauber, Patricia. *Dinosaurs Walked Here.* New York: Bradbury Press, 1987.

Paul, Gregory S. *Predatory Dinosaurs.* New York: Simon & Schuster Inc., 1988.

Steel, Rodney and A. Harvey, eds. *The Encyclopedia of Prehistoric Life.* New York: McGraw-Hill Book Company, 1988.

Stolzenburg, William. "When Life Got Hard," *Science News* (August 25, 1990). pp. 120-121, 123.

Index